Every dramatist's dream: his name and his play's title in lights on a New York marquee, and a line at the box office, even on a rainy day.
(*Theatre Collection, New York Public Library*)